The Haves and Have-Nots

*Guidelines for Leading Congregational Change and
Economically Empowering Poor Communities*

John F. Green, D.Min.

WESTBOW
PRESS®
A DIVISION OF THOMAS NELSON
& ZONDERVAN

Scripture taken from the King James Version of the Bible.

WestBow Press books may be ordered through booksellers or by contacting:

WestBow Press
A Division of Thomas Nelson & Zondervan
1663 Liberty Drive
Bloomington, IN 47403
www.westbowpress.com
1 (866) 928-1240

Because of the dynamic nature of the Internet, any web addresses or links contained in this book may have changed since publication and may no longer be valid. The views expressed in this work are solely those of the author and do not necessarily reflect the views of the publisher, and the publisher hereby disclaims any responsibility for them.

Any people depicted in stock imagery provided by Thinkstock are models, and such images are being used for illustrative purposes only.
Certain stock imagery © Thinkstock.

ISBN: 978-1-5127-7924-0 (sc)
ISBN: 978-1-5127-7926-4 (hc)
ISBN: 978-1-5127-7925-7 (e)

Library of Congress Control Number: 2017903890

Print information available on the last page.

WestBow Press rev. date: 04/24/2017

Dedication

This book is dedicated to my wife, Phyllis, for supporting me in ministry; to my brothers, Henry, Samuel and David for being change agents in the church and community; to my daughter, Courtney and my nephews, G-3.

I express especial thanks to the Bethel African Methodist Episcopal Church in Tallahassee, Florida, whom I served as pastor for twelve years, and afforded me the ministry context for my dissertation that provides the basis for this book.

Personal thanks and appreciation to Drs. Barbara Cotton and Rosalie Hill; Mrs. Jane Jelks Jones and Rev. Rae Fitch for their contributions to this book.

Contents

Foreword

Dr. John Green has written a fascinating investigation into the topics of empowerment, stewardship, and, most importantly, leadership. *The Haves and the Have-Nots* will fill a needed niche in the unfolding literature of community empowerment through nonprofit investment. Dr. Green sees the Church as a necessary community partner in the twenty-first century struggle for corporate uplift.

The Haves and the Have-Nots surveys all of the contemporary literature, synthesizes it, and provides a useful synopsis for the reader interested in bringing theory to practice. Dr. Green anchors his understanding of community empowerment in four different foundations. Like the four legs of a stool, Green's examinations of the biblical, theological, and such create a structure for an empowered church to engage and transform its community. The historical examination in this volume is of specific interest to those who study the history of giving in the United States.

Dr. Green's book provides an eight-stage diagnostic and prescriptive model for churches to follow. Congregational leaders can use this resource as a way of examining and preparing their communities for mission. Although all models need to be adjusted for distinctive situations, *The Haves and the Have-Nots* is easily translatable to various ministry contexts. Eager leaders may want to develop a working guide for institutional development in their particular circumstances. Nevertheless, this book provides necessary content for developing an institutional program.

The Haves and the Have-Nots outlines how to influence change in a congregational environment through vision-casting. Dr. Green's work provides helpful models to pastors, lay leaders, adjudicatories, and other ecclesial officials to fashion and align to their ministerial topographies. This book provides much for the earnest leader to consider when working on the project of vision-casting. I commend its use to every congregational leader.

Reverend Michael Joseph Brown, PhD
Academic Dean and Interim President
Payne Theological Seminary
Wilberforce, Ohio

Introduction

According to Marvin McMickle, the black middle-class society has lost "a power balance between social activities, their spiritual commitments to the Church, and the need to assume some responsibility for those persons still confined to the inner-cities who need the very help and expertise possessed in abundance by the black middle-class." However, it is ironic that in the quest for social status, some middle-class blacks view their membership in the church as a social statement. Indicating, somewhere along the road to achieving status, they have, according to Cornell West, become more deficient and are "unlikely candidates for accomplishing the kind of work that must take place in the neighborhoods where there are black middle-class churches."

Thus, the problem confronting middle-class black congregations is the truth about the second great commandment to "love thy neighbor as thyself," and in the process, broadening its awareness and deepening its understanding of the concept of stewardship as a spiritual lifestyle rather than a ceremonial activity.

Black middle-class churches throughout the nation have a spiritual, moral, and church mandate to assist and help empower the blacks that have not found a way out of poverty or neighborhoods and lifestyles that keep them economically disadvantaged.

In recent years, the black community served by the black church experienced significant social and economic change. These changes can be attributed to a period of national prosperity, the Civil Rights Movement, and Affirmative Action legislation, which brought about increased income. The changes enhanced the ability of blacks to make personal decisions about where to go to school and where to live. Consequently, an increased number of blacks, based on improved job levels, higher educational attainment, and improved lifestyles, acquired "black middle-class status." This improved lifestyle allowed a significant number of blacks to relocate to the suburbs. Therefore, unfortunately, many are no longer an integral part of the immediate black community where the black church resides, though many still travel back to the black community to worship.

While there is a rising number of middle-class blacks across this nation, considered to be among the "haves," there is, unfortunately, a significant number of blacks still living in low-cost housing and underserved neighborhoods with low property values—the "have-nots." They continue to attend substandard schools, earn wages at the poverty level, and experience all of the inequities and struggles that result from a poor quality of life. The blight of this population sends out a serious message to the black church as it tests the realness of the black church's theology and spirituality.

In the chapters to follow, I shall examine the biblical, theological, historical, and theoretical warrants for economically empowering the poor, establish a leadership model for affecting congregational change toward economic empowerment, and review models of ministries engaged in economic empowerment.

Some sociologists imply that the black church has been and continues to be the only institution available to service the needs of the black community because it is an independent institution. It is the institution that nurtures and cares for the black community. However, given the black population transition, according to Malone, "there is a question about whether it still serves as the center for economic, social and intellectual life of the black community." A question I hope to resolve in the subsequent chapters.

Chapter 1

Empowering the Poor: Biblical, Theological, Historical, and Theoretical Foundations for a Ministry of Economic Empowerment

There is a wide range of biblical and theological foundations that undergird the church's involvement in outreach ministries. Additionally, churches that espouse the tenants of Christ have historically been engaged in community outreach and/or economic empowerment. Moreover, theoretical notions about leadership provide additional insight into issues that help promote a healthy organization (i.e., one that effectively achieves its goals and expected outcomes). This chapter reviews these foundations as a basis for justifying the need to affect change given the status of the contextual organization.

Biblical Foundations for Economic Empowerment

The biblical foundation for a ministry of economic empowerment can be found in the following passages of scripture.

"So when they had come together, they asked him, 'Lord, is this the time when you will restore the kingdom to Israel?' He replied, 'It is not for you to know the times or periods that the Father has set by his own authority. But you will receive power when the Holy Spirit has come upon you; and you will be my witnesses in Jerusalem, in all Judea and Samaria, and to the ends of the earth." (Act 1:6-8 New Revised Standard Version).

This text describes the ministry Jesus passed on to His disciples. He instructed them to be His witnesses in Jerusalem, Judea, Samaria, and to the uttermost parts of the earth. We should notice that in addition to being advised on what to do, Jesus also tells us where He wants us to do the work. This suggests that the black church must go beyond its comfort zone and move outside its walls to places where the church can be witnesses of the liberating and reconciling gospel of Jesus Christ. Inherent in this commission to be witnesses is the challenge to leave the security of the church's wall and go out into the streets of the inner city, where many people are living in poverty. The black church's commitment and programs of ministry must reflect its understanding of what it means to be the Lord's witnesses in Jerusalem, Judea, Samaria, and the uttermost parts of the earth. An understanding of this mission thus prepares the people of the church to develop programs and ministries that will empower and address the needs of the poor in underserved communities.

"You are the salt of the earth" (Matt. 5:13 New International Version) states Jesus in this passage known as the Beatitudes. The way Jesus imagines His disciples as the salt of the earth provides an excellent blueprint for ministry possibilities to black middle-class churches in inner-city communities. In the ancient Near East, salt was not used to season food simply in order to enrich the taste. More importantly, salt was a preservative that prolonged the life of food and helped to delay, if not avoid, its decay. By using the analogy of the church as the salt of the earth, Jesus clearly challenged His disciples to enrich the quality of life for the people who came into contact with them. The black church then meets the challenge of enriching the lives of the poor when it creates a ministry to solve the problems of impoverished communities.

In Luke 16: 19–31, we read the story of the rich man and Lazarus from the perspective of the victim.

> [19] "There was a rich man who was dressed
> in purple and fine linen and who feasted

sumptuously every day. [20] And at his gate lay a poor man named Lazarus, covered with sores, [21] who longed to satisfy his hunger with what fell from the rich man's table; even the dogs would come and lick his sores. [22] The poor man died and was carried away by the angels to be with Abraham.[g] The rich man also died and was buried. [23] In Hades, where he was being tormented, he looked up and saw Abraham far away with Lazarus by his side.[h] [24] He called out, 'Father Abraham, have mercy on me, and send Lazarus to dip the tip of his finger in water and cool my tongue; for I am in agony in these flames.' [25] But Abraham said, 'Child, remember that during your lifetime you received your good things, and Lazarus in like manner evil things; but now he is comforted here, and you are in agony. [26] Besides all this, between you and us a great chasm has been fixed, so that those who might want to pass from here to you cannot do so, and no one can cross from there to us.' [27] He said, 'Then, father, I beg you to send him to my father's house— [28] for I have five brothers—that he may warn them, so that they will not also come into this place of torment.' [29] Abraham replied, 'They have Moses and the prophets; they should listen to them.' [30] He said, 'No, father Abraham; but if someone goes to them from the dead, they will repent.' [31] He said to him, 'If they do not listen to Moses and the prophets, neither will they be convinced even if someone rises from the dead'" (Luke 16:19-31 New Revised Standard Version).

It is one of Luke's more colorful passages on the need to show mercy on the economically less fortunate. Also, it indicates role reversal and a sign of God's judgment against those unwilling to share or show mercy. It places a challenge upon black middle-class churches with regard to their stewardship. How we use our resources in black middle-class churches to solve the problems of the economically disadvantaged who reside outside the church doors bears with it a serious consequence. The passage suggests that our attitude and behavior toward the poor will determine with whom we will be identified. To those in society who have acquired certain advantages, there is a moral obligation and responsibility to help those who are disadvantaged and in poverty. Therefore, by creating ministries of economic empowerment to address the needs of the poor, the black church demonstrates discipleship and stewardship in accordance with biblical warrants for mission and outreach.

Biblical Foundations for Giving

What does the Bible say about giving? In 2 Corinthians 9:6–7, the Apostle Paul tells us that the more one gives, the more one receives. He therefore links generosity with spiritual benefits. Paul writes:

> "Remember this: Whoever sows sparingly will reap sparingly, and whoever sows generously will also reap generously. Each of you should give what he has decided in his heart to give, not reluctantly or under compulsion, for God loves a cheerful giver" (2 Cor. 9:6-7 New International Version).

In this passage, Paul is indicating that one's attitude toward giving determines one's behavior. A person's generosity toward others is a reflection of one's attitude. In like manner, Luke 21:1-4 teaches us a lesson on generous and sacrificial giving by relating the story of the poor widow:

> "He looked up and saw rich people putting their gifts on the treasury; he also saw a poor widow put in two copper coins. He said, 'Truly I tell you, this poor widow has put in more than all of them; for all of them have contributed out of their abundance, but she out of her poverty has

put in all she had to live on'" (Luke 21:1-4 New Revised Standard Version).

According to biblical author Thomas Nelson, the important thing to consider is that two coins were all that the widow possessed. She was definitely destitute, a person who would later qualify for support from the church based on the implied instructions contained in 1 Timothy 5:5;

> "The widow who is really in need and left all alone puts her hope in God…" (1 Tim. 5:5 New International Version).

Although the widow in Luke 21:1–4 could not afford it, she gave generously to the temple. Jesus praised her faithfulness, even though it was a great sacrifice. In praising the attitude of the widow, Jesus shows the attitude of God by not paying attention to the amount, but as Nelson points out, he pays more attention to her attitude in giving.[1]

What seems to be a constant pattern for Jesus in scripture is his preoccupation with one's attitude toward giving, which is again the case in Mark 14:4–7;

> "But some were there who said to one another in anger, 'Why was the ointment wasted in this way? For this ointment could have been sold for more than three hundred denarii and the money

given to the poor.' And they scolded her. But, Jesus said, 'Let her alone; why do you trouble her? She has performed a good service—for you always have the poor with you, and you can show your kindness to them whenever you wish; but you will not always have me'" (Mark 14:4-7 New Revised Standard Version).

Unlike the disciples, who displayed concern with seemingly the waste of the woman's generosity, Jesus displays concern with the attitude of her giving. While the disciples viewed the extravagance of her gift as taking food away from the poor, Jesus looked upon her gift as an act of worship. This passage brings to question the issue of how one's use of material wealth can be considered a part of worship. What act of worship might we give while we have the opportunity? How might we honor the Lord materially? Although these are difficult questions to answer, they are critically important questions for consideration in the black middle-class church. But again, the scripture provides us with insight. In Mark 14:6, Jesus told His disciples that just as the woman had done Him a "good service," they could do "good" to the poor at any time. In other words, though Jesus is not physically among us, we can worship God with the generosity of giving by using our resources to help meet the needs of the poor.

Biblical Foundations for the Church's
Role in Empowering the Poor

The church is faced with the opportunity daily to do a good work for the poor. When we give to the poor, we honor the Lord. Therefore, in considering the influence attitude has upon behavior, it appears that change in attitude toward worship may be a good place to begin in the black middle-class church. Some questions for later consideration may include the following: What kind of understanding do members of the black middle-class church have about their worship of God? Does this understanding, or perhaps misunderstanding, relate in any way to giving support to the poor?

In referring to Christ's statement "You have the poor with you always," Rus Walton in his book, *Biblical Solutions to Contemporary Problems* proposes that Christ did not give the task of caring for the poor to the government.[2] He suggests that this task was given to Christ's sheep, His church. But the problem, says Walton, is that the church has not done a very good job with caring for the poor.

Why has the church failed in this task? In the writer's opinion, the church in general and the black middle-class church in particular have become too comfortable with the government providing social programs for the community to meet the needs of the poor. Consequently, the church, for the most part, does not consider caring for the poor one of its major obligations. This notion, which seems to dominate the attitudes of most middle-class black churches, must be changed and the church must again resume responsibility for its work, which is based in scripture.

Because the generosity of the church is often abused, how can the church determine the deserving poor? Walton uses the following biblical references as a guide: "Not the slothful" (Prov. 24:30-34 New International Version) "Not the sluggard" (Prov. 21:25–26 New International Version), and "Not the person who can but will not work" (2 Thess. 3:10 New Revised Standard Version). Walton firmly states, "Biblical law severely condemns the lazy and the wasteful and the irresponsible."[3] He cautions, however, that the Bible is equally harsh on those who fail to help the poor. Using Exodus 22:22 and Matthew 25:41–46 (New Revised Standard Version), he points out that when it comes to "the deserving poor (the truly needy), the unfortunate, the widow, the abandoned and down-and-out, the church is obligated to provide charity (love) as a part of its life work for Christ." He also suggests that "evangelism is a vital part of the Christ-centered task of reclaiming the destitute and helping them reclaim their lives."[4]

Since our task as Christians is to care for the poor, an attitude of essential mandate, based on biblical foundations, must be developed in black middle-class churches. Recognizing what Christ expects of us enables us to fulfill the tasks of the church on earth. Today, the black middle-class church enjoys a quality lifestyle of financial and material wealth. Marvin McMickle states, "It is unconscionable for the fairly secure members of black middle-class churches to gather once or twice a week for worship and fellowship among themselves and not find effective and creative ways to respond to the socio-economic needs that are found just outside their doors."[5] How can black middle-class churches respond to the needs that exist just beyond their doors? McMickle suggests that the answer can be found in Luke 16:20-21:

> "And at his gate lay a poor man named Lazarus covered with sores who longed to satisfy his hunger with what fell from the rich man's table°…" (Luke 16:20-21 New Revised Standard Version).

For those with much, like the rich man, we must decide how responsible we are for the poor. The passage seemingly implies that we are greatly responsible because our neglect of the poor has consequences of Godly judgment. Therefore, members of the black middle-class churches must picture themselves as the rich man and deserving poor in communities around "the rich man's door", as Lazarus. If we fail to respond, like the rich man, to the needs of the poor, then we too in black middle-class churches must face the judgment of God. This passage serves as the challenge to members in black middle-class churches to recognize our discipleship and stewardship in the world. The black middle class can no longer consider it Christian to neglect the needs of the poor. To neglect the poor is to neglect our responsibilities as Christians to serve as the hands, the feet, and the eyes of Jesus and to demonstrate Jesus's compassion. Exemplifying an attitude of generosity, concern, and care for the poor is the task of the church in general and the black middle-class church in particular. Giving to the poor must be looked upon as an act of worship, an opportunity to give to God. Therefore, black middle-class churches must spare no expense in carrying out this mandate proclaimed in scripture.

Theological Foundations for Economic Empowerment

A theological warrant for a ministry of empowerment for the economically poor in the black church is found in the doctrine of human beings. Within this doctrine, we are taught that to be human is to depend not only on God, but also on one another. As human beings, we need one another's help. But in our attempt to help others, we must be careful not to play God. We accomplish this effort by first recognizing that the help we give anyone is very limited. In other words, it is impossible for us to know exactly what another person needs. At best, we can only guess at giving him or her what help we can with the understanding that we are human beings and not God. Therefore, in the black church's effort to empower the economically poor, it must be understood that the most that can be done in many cases is to stand by the poor in their need and provide them with whatever assistance is humanly possible.

The doctrine of the attributes of God also provides an understanding. When we understand God's loving justice, then we are able to lay a foundation for giving the poor what they need. Within the doctrine of the attributes of God, justice is usually understood to mean the fair and equal treatment of all people. Throughout the Bible there are vivid pictures of God's justice and mercy in matters pertaining to people who are politically and economically poor and oppressed by those who are secure with power and wealth. The black church, like God, must take up the cause of the poor because they lack political and economic power. How can the black church do this? By identifying with the poor and being an advocate for the poor. Therefore, the black church must recognize the political and social forces that place people in economic deprivation. By exposing these forces and working to disarm them, the church can use its political and economic power to liberate the poor from continued oppression.

The Christian doctrine of providence provides underlying theological considerations. This doctrine hinges on God's presence in people who love enough to risk their own comfort and security to be of service to another person. It suggests that, when given an opportunity to help others, we are invited to be instruments of God's providential care by our willingness to minister to other people in this way. So we are taught through this doctrine that God has given us an invitation not to escape but to deliberately accept the suffering of others—the suffering that inevitably comes when we stand with, by, and for others who suffer.

By accepting the invitation not to escape the suffering of the poor, the black church must demonstrate its care through the providence of the God who delivered Israel from bondage and raised Jesus from the dead; the God who is so powerful that evil must finally serve His goodwill for our sake. In other words, the church must believe that something good can come out of crime-infested communities, drug-ridden and violent streets, and economically and politically deprived neighborhoods. If the black church becomes God's instrument, this action enables those considered underpowered or marginalized to live in hope for the future even when present experiences seem to offer no hope.

Theological Basis for Giving

Thomas Jeavons and Rebekah Basinger quote James Hudnut Beumler's belief of "three alternative theological understandings of giving that emerged out of the Protestant Reformation. First is Martin Luther's conception of giving as an act of thanks for God's unmerited grace. Second is John Calvin's view of the disposition of material resources as stewardship over something that is not ultimately of human ownership. Third is the Arminian/Wesleyan understanding of human acts of giving as volitional responses to divine activity." Jeavons and Basinger suggest that the Catholic concept of the "social mortgage" is added to the three. This concept holds that all of one's material possessions are produced by the efforts of the people—that the entire community is responsible for one's wealth. But they propose that no one concept should take preference over another because they each contribute to a holistic interpretation of the commonality of faith and possessions.[6]

Lovett H. Weems Jr. states, "John Wesley was clear on the unity of faith and action." Often called a folk theologian, Wesley wrote:

"Christianity is essentially a social religion, and to turn it into a solitary religion is indeed to destroy it."[7]

Wesley's personal life serves as a testimony to the Christian's obligation to advance the welfare of others and was an inspiration to the early Methodists. He believed that money was a good servant but a bad master. Thus, he chose to use his own money to serve others by literally giving away most of his income over the years. Because of his concern for the poor, for five consecutive days in the middle of winter an eighty-plus-year-old Wesley walked the streets of London from morning till evening, ankle deep in melting snow, raising nearly a thousand dollars "to clothe them that needed it most." To Wesley, poverty was a social concern. He believed that it resulted from a misuse of community resources. Wesley's views about poverty stemmed from his theological understanding of God as owner and people as stewards. His position was that irresponsible use of resources, especially frivolous spending on luxuries by the rich, was the reason for so much poverty. And because he saw considerable deprivation in the streets of London, at times he requested government action to relieve the suffering of the poor.

For Wesley, there was no separation of the church from social concerns. He believed that to be Christian was to be socially conscious about the needs of the poor. He preached that the church cannot become so "heavenly-minded" that it is of "no earthly good." The gospel compels Christians to strive for spiritual holiness, but also they must strive for social holiness. As disciples of Jesus Christ, Wesley believed that the church must use its resources to "feed the hungry, clothe the naked," and provide opportunities for the needy to rise up out of poverty. Today, Wesley's folk theology of faith and action is still relevant for addressing the needs of the poor. From his theology, we have a paradigm for the development of an attitude of social holiness within black middle-class churches and becoming a witness to the good work that can be done by the church when it intervenes to lessen the problems of the poor.

Reinhold Niebuhr states, "The moral attitudes of dominant and privileged groups are characterized by universal deception and hypocrisy." In other words, there is an unconscious and conscious identification of their special interest with public view and widespread values. Niebuhr suggests, "The most common form of hypocrisy among privileged classes is the attitude that their privileges are the just payments with which society rewards especially useful or meritorious function."[8] The problem with this type of attitude is, when used by privileged classes who possess hereditary advantages, that it must be proved or assumed that the underprivileged classes would not have the capacity of rendering the same service if given the same opportunity. Niebuhr concludes that "Dominant classes are always slowest to yield power because of the source of privilege. As long as they hold it, they may dispense and share privilege, enjoying the moral pleasure of giving what does not belong to them." Niebuhr further states that the English word *generous* comes from a Latin root *generousus*, which shows that generosity was also considered to be a unique virtue of the privileged. It was Thorsten Vebien, according to Niebuhr, who cynically interprets the generosities of the privileged as efforts to secure the jealousy of others by putting their wealth on display.[9]

According to James Bacik, Niebuhr believed that imbalances in economic and political power produce injustices. He quotes Niebuhr as saying:

> "Special privileges make all men dishonest. The poorest conscience and the clearest mind are prostituted by the desire to prove them morally justified."[10]

Bacik stated that it was Niebuhr's view that "We cannot expect to solve our social problems simply by using reason, education, and moral persuasion, because self-interest and power struggles are inevitably involved in social life."[11] Therefore, in order to solve our social problems, we must make decisions on social questions based on well-thought-out strategies from which actions and policies will create an end result of good over evil. Bacik and Niebuhr reinterpreted various Christian doctrines to support and clarify this pragmatic approach. For example, Niebuhr employed the Reformation notion of justification by faith alone to show that we must involve ourselves in the search for justice even when the present situation is cloudy with despair. Niebuhr's thought rejected simply trust in God's power to save our sinful world and us. Instead, he advocated relying on our own power to solve all human problems by not yielding to the temptation to withdraw from public life because moral choices are not clear and good results are not assured. Because of this view, Bacik suggested, "Niebuhr castigated the great neo-orthodox theologian Karl Barth for advocating a theology which leads to a withdrawal from the real world of power politics." Thus, Niebuhr insisted that the traditional "theology of the cross can strengthen us to face the tragic dimension of life without falling into despair." The cross of Christ creates a framework of meaning, which enables us to work realistically for a better world without expecting perfection. In this regard, Bacik states, "Christianity is especially helpful in dealing with social problems because it reveals to us a God of judgment who condemns injustice, and a God of mercy who frees us to work for a better world."[12] As a model for the pursuit of social justice, Bacik concludes that Niebuhr advocates a practical strategy rather than simply depending on education and social responsibility. The essence of that strategy can be found in these words;

> "The selfishness of human communities must be regarded as inevitability. Where it is inordinate it can be checked only by competing assertiveness of interest; and these can be effective only if coercive methods are added to moral and rational persuasion."[13]

In his examination of Gustavo Gutierrez's theology of social justice, Bacik advances Gutierrez's view that the Christian has not shown enough significant involvement in the cause of social justice. "He [the Christian] has not perceived clearly enough that to know God is to do justice."[14] In other words, Gutierrez believes that there is a temptation among Christians to divorce their understanding of the gospel from the practical concerns of everyday life. Gutierrez advances the theory of a liberating praxis, whereby those who are able would unify and blend their talents and resources to work with the poor and oppressed to bring about the formation of a changed world and a changed disposition of humanity toward the poor.[15] He suggests that this liberating praxis must be at the center of the Christian life.

According to Bacik, Gutierrez's reinterpretation of the notion of salvation in the Bible is the key to the context of his theology. For Gutierrez, "Salvation is an inner-world power, definitely unleashed by Jesus Christ, which transforms and guides the whole unified historical process."[16] Gutierrez says that salvation has its beginnings in the creation of the world by Jesus Christ, who engages human beings into a subordinate relationship and entrusts them with the responsibility of helping to bring history to its fulfillment.

Bacik states that, for Gutierrez and other liberation theologians, the exodus not only makes clear our interpretation of biblical salvation, but it also sheds more light on the church's struggle to create a better world. In the exodus story, salvation must be seen as a permanent historical reality that impacts both the inner life of individuals and the public, social, and economic life of the community, as with confronting issues of conflict and overcoming social injustices. According to Gutierrez, "the Exodus keeps us from spiritualizing" the work of salvation by reducing it to an interior liberation of the soul. In other words, the promise of God's salvation, as expressed in the covenant, touches all areas of life, including the physical as well as the social, spiritual, and personal. In Gutierrez's words:

> "This reminds us that the life of charity today cannot be confined to giving handouts to poor individuals, but must include the effort

to liberate whole groups of people from unjust structures and oppressive systems."[17]

Bacik concludes that the scriptural reinterpretation of the exodus suggested by Gutierrez provides a foundation for the "preferential option for the poor."[18] This means that God, the liberator of the oppressed, identifies with the poor not because they are better, but because of their sorrows and sufferings. Gutierrez interprets the biblical view of material poverty as "a subhuman condition, the fruit of injustice which must be overcome." If this view is to be accepted, the church must develop an attitude of genuine evangelical poverty, a total dependence on God that leads to a life of solidarity with the poor. The church must empower the poor to participate in their own struggle for liberation. They must be taught to become agents of change. According to Bacik, "The preferential options for the poor is not a Marxist idea leading to a welfare state, but a biblically-based notion, which recognizes that the poor have an important part in creating a better world." When the church joins with the poor in the battle against oppressive structures, not only is the church helping the needy, but it's also enriched by the poor in what Gutierrez calls a "two-way evangelism."[19]

Finally, a church choosing to follow the example of Jesus Christ must take the side of the poor. It must be challenged to broaden its understanding of other important Christian doctrines. Jesus Christ must be seen not only as our personal Savior, but also as the liberating Christ.

Historical Foundations for Empowerment of the Poor

A basic historical warrant for a ministry of empowerment for the economically deprived can be traced back to Africa. In Africa, land was always recognized as belonging to the community. This is unlike the capitalist methods of individual ownership of land that we experience in the Western world. Under the tribal community system, everyone had a right to use the land to prevent community poverty. A review of African history teaches that the tribal community operated on the barter system—the exchanging of products and services without the use of money. This practice seems to suggest a form of Christian stewardship that demonstrates a sense of shared responsibility for the economic well-being of everyone living in the tribal community.

Using the traditional African system of economic empowerment, the black church may empower poor communities by setting up a community barter system. Thus, teaching folks to help meet the needs of others through the process of exchanging products and services seems to be a viable process. Identifying who has the skills and what abilities exist and creating ways to share these skills and abilities within the community for the well-being of the community may be an approach to empowering the community.

Another historical warrant stems from the inception of the African Methodist Episcopal Church (AME). Organized in Philadelphia, Pennsylvania, in 1787, the AME Church provided for the socioeconomic empowerment of black people through the creation of self-help programs. Richard Allen, the founder of the AME Church, demonstrated his zeal for economic empowerment by purchasing a blacksmith shop on the corner of Sixth and Lombard Streets in Philadelphia. This establishment was the first real estate owned by black people in the United States. The property is known today as the Mother Bethel African Methodist Episcopal Church.

The AME Church's contributions to the socioeconomic development of black people in the South started with its involvement in the Underground Railroad, which helped to carry slaves to freedom after the emancipation of slaves on January 1, 1863. Further, when importing African Methodism to Florida through the leadership of Charles Pearce, an educated clergy who turned his attention to state and local politics, the AME Church became one of Florida's premier political powers. Shortly after Congress mandated the right to vote to free African Americans in early 1867, the AME

Church led the way for black voters along with northern and southern loyalists to seize control of the Florida government. Incidentally, this was accomplished through the efforts of the Republican Party.

Theoretical Foundations for Stewardship Ministry

Almost unanimously, studies on congregational giving and stewardship express the urgent need for pastors and lay leaders to place emphasis on stewardship as a biblical mandate for all Christians. The implication from these findings is that failure to teach the giving aspect of Christianity through carefully developed programs of stewardship education handicaps the church's ability to economically empower poor communities.

T. Mollegen Jr. has suggested two attitudes toward giving that should be cultivated in the church. One is the program-oriented (or goal-oriented) attitude. This posture motivates one to give out of the desire to see an identified need met; perhaps the purchase of something such as food for the poor, books for the Sunday school, or computers for a learning lab. According to Mollegen, this type of giving can be called mission-motivated or possibly outreach-motivated giving. It occurs when a person is motivated to give to benefit others, demonstrating a behavior grounded in Jesus's summary commandments: "Thou shalt love thy neighbor as thyself°…"

(Luke 10:27 King James Version). Another stewardship attitude presented by Mollegen is giving out of thankfulness and love for God, or nonprogram-motivated giving. This attitude demonstrates that the person is thankful for God's blessings and wishes to demonstrate his or her thankfulness by giving back to God. Here, a person recognizes that everything one has is a gift from God. With the acceptance of this attitude, a person will voluntarily relinquish control over what he or she has to be used for God's purposes.[20]

Giving to support mission can be viewed as being responsive to the second of Jesus's summary commandments. In like manner, nonprogram-motivated giving out of love for God can be viewed as being responsible to the first and greatest of the summary commandments: "Thou shalt love the Lord thy God with all thy heart, all thy soul, and all thy mind, and all thy strength" (Luke 10:27 King James Version). The level of giving required of this commandment is total commitment. Therefore, if the attitudes of members in black middle-class churches are to become mission motivated or motivated by their love of God, this must become the foundation by which pastors teach that Jesus wanted all His followers to help people in need.

According to Eugene Grimm;

> "Stewardship is simply recognizing that all we
> are and all we have is a gift from God. We are
> entrusted with gifts—to care for these gifts, to
> manage them, and to employ them to serve God
> in the world."[21]

But he adds that stewardship does not happen instinctively.
It happens by design. And he believes that as the chief Bible
teacher and theologian, the pastor must build the foundation
for stewardship through the education, grooming, and
leadership of the local congregation.[22]

The idea that stewardship does not occur spontaneously in
the heart of the individual is examined in the Stewardship
Journey Study conducted by the United Methodist Church
Foundation. The study determined that the concept of
stewardship is not always readily accepted. To the contrary,
it is one of the most severe problems faced by American
Christians. This is because the average American, including
the Christian, is in a constant struggle against advertisers,
financial consultants, and others who proclaim that one
must accumulate an abundance of material possessions as
a means of affirming one's self-worth. Thus, the proclivity
toward the use of one's money and possessions as well as one's

talents, time, experiences, and other gifts to bolster one's self-glorification has become an acceptable rule of behavior.

The study proposes that to alter this behavior, pastors and lay leaders must approach stewardship as an element of one's spiritual journey. It suggests that stewardship is a product of growth and maturity, and not all people reach this stage in the spiritual journey at the same time. Nor can we reach this stage alone. "The pastor has to preach it, the teachers have to teach it, the leaders have to lead out and make their gifts first, and the congregation has to celebrate it." Stewardship must be a constant theme that is fundamental to all of the other affairs of the church. Through Bible study, sermons, and other kinds of group study, pastors and lay leaders must help members of congregations develop in their spiritual journeys. They must systematically promote the examples and models of the Old and New Testament that demonstrate how we are to respond to and manage money and things.[23]

Establishing biblical roots of stewardship is an easy charge, as many different images and stories about sharing and giving are written throughout the Bible. This is especially true in terms of the Bible's emphasis on the attitude and use of money. According to Grimm, the fact that sixteen of Jesus's approximately thirty-eight parables dealt with money, and that one of every seven verses in the gospels of Matthew,

Mark, Luke, and John deal in some fashion with money, is evidence that Jesus understood more than we do about the preemptive power of money in the lives of man. [24]

By returning to the biblical basis of stewardship, one can be led to the understanding and appreciation of knowing that stewardship is not secular in nature, that it is not the result of someone's own personal present-day theory. Rather, it is a way of living commanded by God and confirmed by God's Son, Jesus,[25] Pastors and lay leaders must be careful not to treat stewardship education as simply a way to raise money. They must emphasize that its purpose is to help Christians grow in faith and spiritual maturity and is a positive expression to God that one is grateful for one's blessings.[26]

Kennon L. Callahan writes in *Giving and Stewardship in an Effective Church* that establishing a clear vision of mission is essential to developing a congregation's disposition toward giving. This, he says, is the first principle of giving. He suggests that churches must shift the focus from fund-raising to a focus on the eternal mission of the church. This means that churches have the responsibility of not only preaching but also of teaching, healing, nurturing, giving, building, and many other responsibilities in the establishment of God's kingdom on earth. Callahan suggests that if the mission of the church is emphasized and if church initiatives are built around the mission, people will give in support of the mission. And he holds that the more mission is pressed, the more people will give. He bases this action on the premise that most people want to make a difference and want the assurance that they are living for a meaningful cause. Therefore, they are more willing to give to programs directed at making a difference in others' lives. Finally, he concludes that people do not give generously when the emphasis is on simple fund-raising to receive enough money for maintenance or to balance the budget. However, they do give when it can be shown that the church is pursuing specific, concrete mission objectives.

Thomas H. Jeavons and Rebekah Burch Basinger present a similar view. They contend that people of faith tend to value and support significant causes, that "they take deep satisfaction in being part of something that is larger and greater than themselves."[27]

Stan Toler and Elmer Towns agree. They suggest that when given the opportunity to practice the stewardship principles that have been taught them, people will respond willingly. Therefore, they suggest that establishing a vital mission and compassion ministry encourages vital stewardship. Toler and Towns propose that pastors and other stewardship educators challenge Christians by establishing a vision plan, a detailed and realistic picture of the future of the local congregation that will prove God with their giving. Such a plan calls for the development of an environment of constant giving born out of the realization that Christian giving is the way by which God maintains His kingdom on earth and that the congregation wants to play a part in God's plan.[28]

Kennon Callahan proposes that another principle of giving and stewardship is the development in the minds of the people that they are giving to a winning cause. This winning cause is the mission of God. Through His mission, "People will be helped and lives will be changed." Callahan's metaphor, "People give to a winning cause, not a sinking ship," also refers to the kind of leadership model that must exist in order to successfully pursue God's mission. He says that congregations with an attitude of being part of a winning cause have pastors and key leaders who possess the gifts of growing, developing, advancing, and building up the congregation. While leaders who communicate the spirit of a sinking ship are bent toward complaining, lamenting, scolding, and whining.

Leaders who reflect the spirit of a winning cause encourage confidence in and assurance of the mission. They discern opportunities for individuals and groups to move toward innovative possibilities and help them set realistic goals. They push forward in the wake of occasional defeat while continuing to demonstrate confidence in God's mission.

People with these qualities advance the individual's faith as well as the faith of the congregation and help people devote their individual and corporate lives to the mission of God. On the other hand, leaders who reflect the spirit of a sinking ship raise doubts. They consistently complain about how things are not going well with the church finances. They complain that people are not committed. They create a climate of resignation or perhaps anger. This brand of leadership fails to lift up God's mission, and it suppresses a generous and giving attitude.[29]

Grimm also emphasized the importance of leadership in invoking stewardship. In fact, he suggests that leadership is one of the most important considerations in developing a stewardship environment. Grimm stresses that pastors and lay leaders lead best by example. What leaders do has much more of an influence on the congregation than what they say. First, Grimm says, they must be personally committed to Jesus Christ and to the ministry to which they have been called through the church. Second, they must be faithful stewards themselves, committed to giving. Grimm insists that their giving must include willingness toward the biblical principles of percentage giving and tithing. He also suggests that in order to achieve a spirit of stewardship, leaders must exercise leadership dynamics such as being able to discern vision, build consensus, and communicate vision effectively.[30] These and other leadership traits will be examined in chapter 2.

In summary, there is biblical, theological, and historical justification for the black middle-class church to influence positive attitudes and heighten sensitivity to empowering economically poor communities. All indications strengthen the notion that we are indeed our brother's keeper. The scriptures teach us that our mission is to go out into other communities to do all that we can to preserve and prolong the life of others as witnesses for Christ. Moreover, all that we have comes from God, and unless we sacrifice and seek righteousness in the eyes of God, we are subject to risking our real reward, which is in heaven. We have a Christian and a moral obligation to help one another, especially those who are less fortunate. Theologically, our understanding of God's providence helps us to understand the goodness of God that is within us and enables us to respond to the need, identify with and advocate for the less fortunate. Each of us is an instrument of God and must love enough and care enough for others for them to see God through us.

Historically, the need and obligation to help one another and preserve our community was established with our forefathers in Africa. Subsequently, the notion of self-empowerment came to us through Richard Allen and the African Methodist

Church. It has been done before. It can be done again! The church must build on these foundations and further its efforts to empower the economically poor. A guideline for moving further with this notion is found in the next chapter.

Chapter 2

Guides for Church Leadership in Affecting Congregational Change toward Economic Empowerment

It has been clearly revealed that stewardship is not instinctive and that leadership plays a crucial role in invoking stewardship as well as facilitating change. The model for effecting change as espoused by Jim Herrington, Mike Bonem, and James Furr lends itself to leadership as a spiritual gift and the pastor as the leading change agent. Thus, it coincides with this writer's thoughts about the importance of leaders as change agents and his belief that this model will enable the leadership to reflect the spirit of a winning cause.

An Eight-Stage Model

The following eight-stage model for congregational change suggested by Jim Herrington, Mike Bonem, and James Furr illustrates four major concepts of pastoral leadership necessary for affecting congregational change. They are: (1) that leadership is a spiritual gift; (2) that effective church change depends on the acceptance and commitment of the congregation to a common vision; (3) that church leaders must be led by the spirit; and (4) that the pastor's success in leading change is built upon the assistance of other leaders who possess different leadership gifts and styles. The first three stages of the suggested change process are: (1) making personal preparation; (2) creating urgency; and (3) establishing the vision community and are designed to assist the pastor and other key leaders in establishing the need and preparing the congregation for change.[31]

Acknowledging that congregational leadership must be spiritually based, the first stage in Herrington's change process is the personal preparation of the pastor and other key lay leaders by seeking God's direction through intensive prayer, Bible study, and meditation. Herrington suggests that personal preparation of God's chosen leaders is illustrated in the Bible through examples such as Moses, who spent considerable time in the desert prior to leading the Jews out of Egypt, and Nehemiah's constant and intensive use of prayer before and during the rebuilding of Jerusalem. But he submits that the ultimate example of personal preparation is Jesus, who spent more time in personal preparation than He did in His recorded ministry. Herrington suggests "personal preparation, through spending time with God, allows the pastor to acquire a fresh awareness of God's eternal mission for the Church."[32]

Personal preparation also involves self-examination of the pastor's key leaders' own motives, abilities, and weaknesses. Self-assessment helps them determine the direction in which to lead, the kinds of assistance they will need, and the kinds of obstacles they may face. Seeking advice and mentoring from the pastors' peers in the ministry is also encouraged during this first stage in the change process. Through them, pastors can acknowledge and clarify their own doubts and concerns, and their peers and mentors can serve as a source of encouragement and challenge.[33] The significance of personal preparation, suggests Herrington, is summed up in Paul's letter to the church in Corinth:

> "Run in such a way as to get the prize. Everyone who competes in the games goes into strict training. They do it to get a crown that will

not last; but we do it to get a crown that will last forever" (1 Cor. 9:24-25 New International Version).

The second stage in Herrington's process of change is creating urgency. Creating urgency means to bring about a stimulant for change by establishing and clarifying God's ideal with the actual state of affairs in the local church. It is what convinces the congregation that change is absolutely necessary and that the present practice, program, or way of thinking must be called into question. Herrington reminds us that urgency is established throughout the Bible as prophets consistently revealed to the people of Israel how much their behavior, conditions, and ways of thinking represented the abandonment of God's plan for them.[34] He maintains that when sufficient urgency is established, the congregation will begin to ask the question the people asked John the Baptist when he was calling them to right living: "What should we do then?" (Luke 3: 10). When asked in the church, such a question implies that the congregation accepts the need for change. Wellington says that urgency is the stimulant that begins the change process. In order to keep the process moving, however, the need to emphasize the breech between current reality and God's plan for the church remains constant.[35]

Herrington agrees with others who have studied the process of change within the church, advocating that the pastor, acting alone, cannot successfully effect change. Rather, he or she must call and depend on assistance from the body of believers. Consequently, the third step in this change process is the establishment of what he calls a vision community. The vision community's focus of attention is on vision, which is structured by and limited to the eternal mission of the church. Its role is to assist the pastor in perceiving and forming the vision, communicating it to the congregation, and formulating and carrying out the concrete measures necessary to achieve the vision. It helps the pastor in guiding the church to where God wants it to be. In doing so, however, its members must establish a common passion, a sense of oneness, mutual interest, and confidence in and reliance on one another to sustain them through the change process. The vision community should reflect the makeup of the congregation. Ideally, it should consist of staff and key lay leaders with contrasting gifts and talents and diversity in age, gender, length of membership, and a cross-representation of ministries. Like the pastor, members of the vision community must engage in personal preparation. They must also recognize the sense of urgency and acknowledge the need for change.[36]

Herrington is careful to emphasize that the vision community works in concert with the pastor. It must not negate the pastor's role as primary leader. In most cases, the pastor would maintain his authority and influence that is his by virtue of his position as the head of the local church. However, the pastor may function on par as a regular member of the vision community and relinquish his or her leadership to a layperson. Whatever the nature of the relationship between the pastor and vision community, it should be based on the policy and pattern of behavior of the local church.[37]

Discerning the vision and the vision path is the fourth stage of Herrington's change process and should also be led by the senior pastor and the vision community. He defines vision as a specific direction in which God is calling a particular congregation to go, and it must evolve from the eternal mission of the church. Vision path is a specific, step-by-step account of how the vision will be accomplished. Herrington proposes that vision, as applied to the church, is different from vision in the secular sense. He maintains that just as God revealed His will for the people to scriptural leaders such as Moses, Samuel, and Paul, God also imbues congregational leaders with the ability to perceive a clear direction for the church.

Herrington proposes that in order to effect change, vision must possess three essential components. It must be "clear, shared, and compelling."[38] He explains that unless vision is capable of being understood, neither leaders nor members will be able to respond to it. If vision is not shared, dissension and counterproductive behavior will weaken the church's ability to extend vigorous effort in response to it. And, if vision is not compelling, it will not inspire the passion and zeal required for the sustained effort and support of the congregation. A clear, shared, and compelling vision is a necessary antecedent for change because it generates support of the congregation and mobilizes it into action. Herrington insists that congregations are becoming less inclined to actively support the pastor simply because of his or her position as head of the church. Rather, in order to achieve and maintain an enthusiastic following, pastors must possess the ability to perceive vision and establish commitment to the church from all segments of the congregation.[39]

Step five, communicating the vision, is a pivotal step in the change process. Up to now, only the senior pastor, his or her staff, and the vision community have been involved in the change process. Communication has been conducted on a one-on-one basis, following carefully constructed rules and procedures. Due to the relatively small size and conjoined nature of this group, differences in opinion and misinterpretation of plans and other issues have been resolved with minimal difficulty. Communicating the vision to the congregation is the beginning of a much more complex process. It involves engaging the congregation in an ongoing process of listening, understanding, accepting, and committing to the vision. Failure to effectively communicate the vision can slow down or even destroy the change process.[40]

Carefully pacing the communication of the vision is also crucial. The pastor and the vision community must be conscious of the fact that the congregation has not been involved in the intricate process of prayer, self-examination, study, and exchange that led to the formulation of the vision. Therefore, it needs time to understand and embrace it in its entirety. Also, Herrington points out that because individuals absorb information in different ways and at different rates, creativity and frequency of communication are critical.[41]

In communicating the vision, Herrington proposes that pastors and key leaders follow the example of Jesus, who he describes as "the master communicator." He writes that Jesus's teachings were unhurried and repetitive by design. Jesus "taught his followers with parables and patient expectations, Old Testament prophecies, and actions. He repeated his central theme over and over without using the exact same words. Christ knew that we would not fully grasp his message immediately upon hearing it and we [pastors and lay leaders] should strive to have the same patience and persistence with today's listeners."[42]

Effective communication of the vision is essential to the change process because it generates greater understanding and commitment of the congregation, produces extensive, vigorous support of the change process, establishes a formal procedure for examining programs and ministries by connecting them to the vision, provides the pertinent information the congregation needs to relieve its fears of and resistance to change, and assists members in recognizing the role they play in the church's future.[43]

The sixth step in Herrington's change process is empowering change leaders. This step is especially challenging because it involves the act of offering leadership roles and assignments to committed members of the congregation other than the senior pastor and a small number of lay leaders and eliminating the barriers that might prevent new leaders from carrying out their functions. Herrington reasons that the pastor and a small group of leaders cannot successfully do a significant change of an enduring congregation. Rather, it requires a wide variety of trusted congregational members who meld the spiritual gifts that God has given them to accomplish the vision of the church. Unlike corporations, Herrington suggests that churches do not routinely seek to identify, train, mentor, and maintain a sufficient reservoir of leaders to carry out the work of the congregation. He advises that churches should routinely foster the growth of leadership through teaching and training.

Then, they should grant leaders sufficient official authority to carry out the function(s) for which they exist.[44] Such an arrangement requires the formulation of a climate that allows individual leaders the freedom to make decisions and to freely introduce and try out new procedures, policies, schedules, and other preparatory activities necessary for the implementation of vision. Herrington refers to this as creating a "permission-giving culture" within the church.[45]

The seventh stage of the change process, implementation, involves the performance of multiple predetermined, strategic procedures and initiatives that are specifically designed to accomplish God's vision for the church. Implementation is directly related to the vision path and is accomplished by the priorities established by the vision community. Once again, the assignment of implementation responsibilities must be carefully matched with the spiritual gifts, interests, and skills of individuals designated to carry out the plan. Implementation, like stages two and five—maintaining a sense of urgency and communicating the vision—is interminable. While specific programs and efforts will be altered and new ones started, Herrington urges that the church should always be in a state of engaging in new creative attempts to accomplish its vision.[46]

The eighth and final step in Herrington's change process is the establishment of momentum and alignment. Alignment occurs "when the majority of the people, ministries, and structures of the Church are functioning out of a clear understanding and commitment to the vision." This stage is also characterized by a common feeling of elation and assurance that the church is following the direction that God has designed for it.[47]

Although maintaining momentum and alignment of the congregation is the last step in Wellington's change process, he emphasizes that it is not the end of the process. Rather, it represents the continuous work that a congregation is called on to perform to carry out God's vision and respond to the needs of a changing world.[48]

The Role of Leadership in Affecting Congregational Change

As evidenced in chapter 1, the need for believers to care for the poor is a constant theme in scripture. In Acts 4: 34-35 Paul clearly defines what the attitude of the early church should be in responding to the needs of others. Paul writes:

> ". . .there were no needy persons among them.
> For from time to time those who owned land
> or houses sold them, brought the money from
> the sales, and put it at the apostle's feet, and

it was distributed to anyone who had need"
(Acts 4:34-35 New International Version).

While God is not calling on today's Christians to sell all their possessions and give the money to the poor, there is no doubt that He expects us to share our possessions (time, talent, and treasure) to help the needy and to provide opportunities for them to improve their conditions. Deuteronomy 15:11 tells us "there will always be poor people in the land" (Deut. 15:11) Therefore, it seems logical that the church's response in attending to the needs of the poor is valid for all times and should be one of its prominent and perpetual functions. Congregations should continually ask themselves, "Who are the poor in the community?" and "How can we reach and help them?" But recent research reveals that this is not happening in many of today's churches; that giving in the church to support programs for social and economic reform has reached a thirty-one year decline.[49] This current state of affairs is clearly alien to God's will for the church. How can this trend be reversed and replaced with a giving and helpful church environment?

Alan Nelson and Gene Appel write in *How to Change Your Church Without Killing It* that when something is or is not happening in the church the way God intends it, leadership is the place to look for the source of the problem. They compare leadership in the church with the life-giving qualities of a car battery. If the battery is weak or dead, the car cannot perform to its greatest capacity. Likewise, while leadership is not the only function necessary for the healthy functioning of the church, Nelson and Appel insists, "It is by far, the most important in an effective improvement [change] process."[50]

Nelson and Appel define leaders as "people who help create, manage and develop change within groups." The operative word is *change*. With this definition in mind, a literature review was conducted with the following two questions in mind: (1) What is the pastor's role in leading change in the church? and (2) What is the process for effecting congregational change? The review of literature revealed common consensus on four major elements of church leadership and change: (1) that unlike general leadership, leadership in the church is a spiritual gift and should be exercised accordingly, (2) that successful leadership in the church must be based on scriptural principles and biblical models, (3) that change within the church can only be accomplished when the leaders and all components of the congregation recognize, accept, and become committed to God's will (vision) for it, and (4) that while the pastor must lead the congregation toward spiritual readiness and recognition of God's vision for the church, acting alone, the pastor cannot bring about change. Shared congregational leadership is necessary to effect significant and lasting congregational change.

The Spiritual Basis for Pastoral Leadership

Henry and Richard Blackaby suggest that to be successful in leading change, the pastor must first recognize and adhere to those principles of leadership that do not apply to the secular leader. First, pastors or spiritual leaders must operate under the firm belief that God directs them to "move people from where they are to where God wants them to be." To accomplish this responsibility, they must recognize and understand God's vision for the church. Then, with conscious effort, they must "move their followers from following their own agendas to pursuing God's purposes."[51]

Second, unlike secular leaders, pastors cannot function under the assumption that they are in control, because they rely solely on the direction of the Holy Spirit. They must recognize that they work in a contradictory mode in that "God calls them to do something that, in fact, only God can do." Therefore, they cannot bring about spiritual transformation within the congregation. Only the Holy Spirit can do this. Thus, they must operate under the posture that they are mere conduits through which the Holy Spirit effects spiritual change.[52]

Third, pastors are not placed in their positions by the people (congregation). They are appointed by God. Therefore, they are accountable to God. And they should not consider themselves to have successfully carried out God's charge to them as leaders until they have moved the people to God's will.[53]

Fourth, pastors must operate from God's agenda and not their own. Often, they mistakenly assume that their position entitles them to establish what should be done. Thus, they pray and ask God's blessings and support of their plans. Blackaby and Blackaby maintain that this assumption is the overlying impediment to effective pastoral leadership. They submit that sound pastoral leadership requires the pastor to seek God's will first and then mobilize the people to follow it.[54]

Robert L. Domokos further emphasizes the spiritual nature of pastoral leadership by qualifying the personal attributes the pastor must possess. He suggests that although skill and experience are required, effective pastoral leadership depends on the extent to which the pastor is Spirit-filled and Spirit-led. He writes that the spiritual life of the local church is intensely affected by the spiritual life of the pastor. The statement "Everything rises and falls on leadership" is particularly applicable to the spiritual life of the church. Consequently, according to Domokos, the pastor, as leader, must model the character of Christ, and his or her ministry must focus on Christ's person and Christ's work. His or her leadership must be distinguished by love, compassion, constraint, and humility. And he or she must provide "spiritual organization, and spiritual drawing power in the church."[55] Domokos offers Acts 20:28 as a scriptural guide for pastors:

> "Take heed, therefore, unto yourselves, and to all the flock over which the Holy Ghost hath made you overseers, to feed the Church of God, which He hath purchased with His own blood" (Acts 20:28 King James Version)

But Domokos adds that pastors cannot take heed of others until they first take heed of themselves. In other words, the pastor's ability to lead others spiritually is directly related to his or her own spiritual comprehension and the extent to which he or she puts it into practice.[56]

Further, Domokos insists that the pastor must exercise authoritative leadership. He cautions, however, that being authoritative does not equate with being autocratic. But, unless a pastor has a clear understanding of what he or she is doing and why and where he or she is going, it is difficult to attract a sustained following of rational people. He cites Romans 12:8 to illustrate his position that leadership is one of the spiritual gifts and pastors must be industrious and persistent in executing it: "If it is leadership, let him govern diligently" (Rom. 12:8 New International Version.) However, like Blackaby and Blackaby, Domokos emphasizes that while pastors must exercise authoritative leadership over their churches, they must not forget that it is Jesus Christ who exercises authority over them.[57]

Lastly, Domokos writes that while pastors must lead with authority, they must realize that their leadership is also sacrificial. Because they work closely with people of different personalities and dispositions under a multitude of conditions, pastors are called on to be more perceptive and responsive to the individual and collective needs of the people. The nature of their leadership requires them to be more charitable and forbearing than secular leaders.[58]

Effective Leadership Principles

Studies on pastoral leadership generally conclude that pastors bear the primary responsibility of identifying the need for and motivating change necessary to move the congregation from where it is to where God wants it to be (*Christian Century* 2001; Blackaby 2001; Domokos 1990; Krejcir 2000; Brown 1999; Nelson and Appel 2000).

However, Nelson and Appel suggest that there is a dearth of effective pastoral leadership in today's churches. Their position is that the average pastor is adept at teaching, preaching, and nurturing but not leading. They further assert that while many pastors may be gifted as managers, leaders are needed to create and perpetuate change.[59] Nelson and Appel's position can be better understood by considering the distinction between managing and leading by Peter Coutts, which focuses on secular organizations but also has great promise for religious organizations. Coutts maintains that since the difference between the principles of management and leadership are not always understood in the broader society, it is not expected to be understood in the life of the church where principles of leadership must also be applied. The following paired contrasts of the characteristics of manager and leader, quoted by Coutts, were taken from *Learning to Lead: A Workbook on Becoming a Leader* by Warren Bennis (1997):

- The **manager** administers; the **leader** innovates.

- The **manager** maintains; the **leader** develops.

- The **manager** accepts reality; the **leader** investigates it.

- The **manager** focuses on systems and structures; the **leader** focuses on people.

- The **manager** relies on control; the **leader** inspires trust.

- The **manager** has a short-range view; the **leader** has a long-range perspective.

- The **manager** asks how and when; the **leader** asks what and why.

- The **manager** has his or her eye on the bottom line; the **leader** has his or her eye on the horizon.

- The **manager** imitates; the **leader** originates.

- The **manager** accepts the status quo; the **leader** challenges it. [60]

According to Bennis, to manage means to conduct, to accomplish, or to have charge of a responsibility while leadership means to originate, to motivate, and to influence the direction of an idea or course of action. Given the differences between management and leadership as determined by Bennis, Coutts suggests that pastors seeking change in the life of a congregation should be prompted to ask themselves questions such as: "Are we being responsive to our community?" "What does our faith call us to be?" "Are we living these qualities out here?" "What do we want our legacy to be to those who follow us?"[61] Nelson and Appel insist, however, that not all pastors have the wide range of gifts and abilities required to lead the change that such questions would generate. Therefore, they "are apt to either avoid change efforts, feel intimidated by lay leaders who promote change initiatives, or bungle improvement projects because they do not understand the leadership process." They further insist that when pastors who are not equipped to understand and implement leadership principles lead congregations, they promote status quo ministry or inconsequential change that falls short of radical or substantial transformation.[62]

Richard Krejcir also ascribes to the view that many pastors are not naturally equipped or adequately prepared for leadership. However, he proposes that leadership skills can be learned. Moreover, he supports the position advocated in other studies that leadership responsibilities can and should be shared with "other godly and capable people." In fact, Krejcir suggests that pastors should carefully evaluate their own abilities and gifts and the abilities and gifts of other church leaders and members. Then they should work within their own gifts and allow other church leaders to operate within theirs. He concludes, "Ministry must be shared through training and encouraging primary leaders, who, in turn, train and encourage secondary leaders, and so forth."[63]

Bill Hybels agrees with Krejcir's view of shared congregational leadership. He notes that the challenges of leadership require many different approaches. Accordingly, he identified ten manifestations of the leadership gift he has observed as needed and performed in the church. These categories of leadership gifts correlate with Bennis's portrayal of the leader as contrasted with manager—that the leader must be adept at innovating, developing, investigating, attracting a following, inspiring trust, and discerning future needs. Hybels emphasizes, however, that one person will not possess all of these manifestations of leadership. Therefore, he proposes the building of teams consisting of leaders with various leadership gifts. Like Krejcir, Hybels maintains that the pastor must identify his or her own leadership gifts and those of his staff and key lay leaders and work within them.[64]

One kind of church leader Hybels has identified is the visionary leader. He writes that the visionary leader has a clear vision of what needs to be achieved and is capable of exercising prolonged and labored effort to achieve the vision. Visionaries are not reluctant to seek the assistance of others and will do what is necessary to keep the vision before the people. Visionary leaders are "future-oriented, usually idealistic, and full of faith to believe that the vision can and will be actualized if the dream is talked about and cast often enough." Hybels says that it is difficult to dissuade visionary leaders. To the contrary, they seem to become invigorated when discouraged. Visionaries may not have leadership qualities such as being able to marshal talent to organize and direct an effort. But, they bear the vision, share the vision, and God gives them the "faith, the power, the people, and the resources" to pursue the vision in spite of obstacles.[65]

Hybels writes that churches also benefit by the presence of directional leaders. The directional leader has the God-given ability to make critical choices when the congregation faces a serious crossroad and is confronted with delivering decisive answers to questions such as: "Is it time for a wholesale change, or should we stay the course? Do we focus on growth or consolidation? Should we start new ministries or deepen and improve existing ones?" Hybels identifies such questions as examples of directional concerns and suggests that they can slow down or inactivate a congregation. However, a directional leader has the ability to weigh the choices that are presented. He or she can assess the values, mission, strengths, weaknesses, resources, personnel, and openness to change of the congregation and then with remarkable wisdom point that organization in the right direction. Directional leaders are–extremely important, Hybels declares, because at such critical times, a wrong move can destroy a congregation. He uses the biblical example of Rehoboam to illustrate how important it is for the leader to be able to gauge the mood of the congregation:

> "Shortly after Solomon's death, his son Rehoboam became king. His first critical intersection came almost immediately: a representative group of the people asked for their workloads to be reduced. Solomon had worked people to the point of despair. Rehoboam had to make a directional call. The older counselors said, "You'd better ease up on them." The younger counselors said, "Just load them up." He made the wrong call at that intersection, and it wrecked the kingdom"[66] (1 Kings 12 New Revised Standard Version).

The strategic leader has the God-given ability to identify the essential procedures needed to achieve the church's vision. Hybels theorizes that people are more likely to be inspired to buy into the vision if they can be shown that it is achievable. The strategic leader can establish consensus among the different units of the congregation and focus their attention on the steps necessary to achieve the vision.[67]

While Hybels recognizes the differences between leadership and management, he suggests that the ability to manage is one of the leadership gifts. Some individuals have the ability to mobilize, coordinate, and regulate the conduct or operation of human and physical resources, procedures, and processes necessary to accomplish the vision. These individuals are managing leaders. And, according to Hybels, although they may not achieve as much recognition as the visionary or directional leader, they are essential for day-to-day operations. They are needed to get the congregation where it wants to go. Hybels offers Old Testament examples of Joseph and Nehemiah as managing leaders.[68]

Churches need motivational leaders also. They are those who have the God-given ability to cast enlivening or exalting influence on members of the congregation that allows it to be continually inspired and excited about the vision. Hybels says that the motivational leader can recognize individual needs. For instance, they can sense who needs "public recognition, an encouraging word, or a day off." He further explains that motivational leaders are aware of and respond to human weaknesses. They know that workers "get tired, lose focus, and experience mission drift." But, when these weaknesses come to bear on the human spirit, motivational leaders know how to encourage and elevate the outlook and disposition of the worker. Jesus was a constant motivator of the disciples.[69]

Then there are shepherding leaders who have the special gift to love, nourish, and support their followers. Their care and concern cultivate kindly feelings and favor in the hearts of those they lead, which helps the church to achieve the vision it sets. Hybels describes the early leadership of David (Samuel 2: 23) as shepherding leadership:

> "He [David] drew together the lonely and disaffected, then shepherded them deeply and lovingly. One night, he happened to mention that he was thirsty, but his troops were surrounded by the enemy. Three members of his team risked their lives to sneak behind enemy lines to bring David a jar of water. When they gave him the water, he was so moved by their expression of love that he poured it out as a worship offering" (2 Sam. 23:15-17 New Revised Standard Version).[70]

Hybels suggests that while many people are attracted to all of the possibilities projected by the visionary leader, many others are drawn to the love and support that they receive from the shepherding leader and will "joyfully pursue almost any kingdom purpose" he or she proposes.[71]

Hybels's team-building leader has the God-given gift to bring people of different abilities and temperaments together to work in harmony toward achieving a common vision. Team-building leaders can match individuals with the jobs or responsibilities that suit his or her special abilities or interests, trusting that each person will pursue his or her specific responsibility while allowing others the freedom to pursue their part of the vision. According to Hybels, team-building leaders may not consider it necessary to nurture or manage. They operate under the premise that as long as "the right people are in the right slots doing the right things for the right reasons, they'll get the work done without the leader looking over their shoulders."[72]

Another kind of leadership that is needed in the church is entrepreneurial leadership. The entrepreneurial leader is inspired by a challenge. He or she enjoys taking risks and is motivated to pursue visions that others deem unachievable. They perform their best when leading start-up programs or projects. However, once a project has been launched, they show no interest in its operational process. Rather, they move on to another challenge. Hybels describes the apostle Paul as an entrepreneurial leader. Paul wanted to establish churches but let others operate them so that he could move on to his next pioneering effort.[73]

Reengineering leaders are important because they have the God-given ability to give new life or vigor to a declining vision or congregation. They establish what the original purpose and needs were and, upon analyzing and assessing existing circumstances, decide what needs to be done. But, like entrepreneurial leaders, reengineering leaders are not interested in conducting, managing, or directing what has been recrafted. They look for new programs or projects to repair or revive.[74]

The final category of church leaders suggested by Hybels is the bridge-building leader. The bridge-building leader has the God-given ability to bring the different elements of the congregation with their varying interests and goals together to pursue a common vision. They are proficient in acquiring the goodwill and confidence of different groups while supporting each group's separate interests. They attempt to connect individual group interests and guide groups through the process of concentrating their efforts on producing the same results. Hybels's conclusion regarding pastoral leadership is that many leadership gifts and styles must be used to lead God's people toward change. One person will not manifest all of these gifts. Therefore, pastors must be able to recognize their individual God-given leadership gifts and styles, lead according to the way God has gifted them, and select other church leaders to assist according to the way God has gifted them.

One other category of leaders not mentioned by Hybels should be given consideration when analyzing pastoral leadership: the thought leader. Kevin A. Miller suggests that the thought leader is important because he or she transforms the mind-set of the congregation without posing a specific agenda. The thought leader leads the people in a Christward direction through preaching and teaching. Thought leaders can be compared to the apostles in Acts 6: 1–4 who left the administrative needs of the early church to carefully selected leaders while they gave their "attention to prayer and the ministry of the word" (Acts 6:4 New International Version), Krejcir refers to the thought leader as the preacher/teacher and proclaims that this really is the pastor's major role, while other leadership roles can be delegated.[75]

Jim Herrington, Mike Bonem, and James Furr express a similar view in proposing that pastors must take the lead in assisting the congregation in renewing and maintaining spiritual and relational vitality. Spiritual vitality means that the people possess a profound feeling of the presence of God and His love in their individual and congregational life. Rational vitality describes the people's unqualified love for others. The scriptural basis for spiritual and relational vitality is expressed in Matthew 22: 37–40, where Jesus gives instruction:

> "Love the Lord your God with all your heart, and
> with all your soul, and with your entire mind.

This is the first and greatest commandment. And the second is like it; Love your neighbor as yourself. All the law and the prophets hang on these two commandments." (Matt. 22:37-40 New International Version)

Herrington proposes that the acceptance of Jesus's commandments to love God and love one's neighbor is the essential force that provides the life-giving power to Christians, which allows them to pursue God's vision for their lives. It is only when the congregation shares this corporate state of mind, or what Miller refers to as a mind-set, that substantial change can be generated. Through worship, prayer, and teaching and through the fostering of a spirit of grace, unity, and community, the pastor invokes the spiritual and relational vitality of the congregation that prepares it to pursue corporate change efforts.[76]

These authors have clearly demonstrated that the God-given leadership gifts of the pastor are important to the change process. Secondly, however, there are many gifts needed to promote substantial transformation. Therefore, the skillset should be shared with other leaders throughout the church. Effecting change could be a dynamic team-building process and as pointed out by Bill Hybels, the right person in the right position, doing the right thing for the right purpose, at the time needed could be a powerful change agent. These findings have great implications for my attempt to outline a plan of strategies to be utilized to effect change in the church.

Meanwhile, chapter 3 provides a look at models and the basis for models that have been used to engage in economic empowerment in the black community.

Chapter 3

Models of Ministries Engaged in Economic Empowerment

Throughout the history of America, people of organized religious communities have grappled with the need for economic empowerment in the black community. Consequently, they have passed on theoretical thinking that still remains with us and can be observed in pockets of the black community even though they are differing views. This, however, gives credence to the fact that the black community is not monolithic in its views about economic empowerment and there are a number of approaches. There is no evidence to support which approach may be more successful than others.

Basic Black Religious Community Models

History records that Richard Allen, the founder of the African Methodist Episcopal Church, brought for the first time in American history a church built on sociological grounds to promote brotherhood and equality along racial lines. It was his interpretation of the second great commandment, "Thou shalt love thy neighbor as thyself"[77] that awakened a new perspective in church ministry.

Embedded in Allen's bold move to establish the African Methodist Episcopal Church was the need to create a ministry, if you will, that caters to the spiritual, social, and economic concerns of African American people. Thus, beginning with the need for social and religious equality and imposing the thrust for self-help, economic empowerment has been a focus of the African Methodist Episcopal Church for more than two hundred years.

According to Walter Malone Jr., the development of economic empowerment programs should be the answer to what we will do with the resources we control in order to contribute to the empowerment of the communities we serve.

Black churches have not been lacking vision, but they may be lacking models to help provide structure and relief for planning with purpose and with relatedness of their vision to the spirit of the black community. Among many, Malone Jr. discusses three schools of thought utilized by three outstanding religious leaders that provide basis for model ministries. They include:

1. Give of Yourself to Self-Development—Separatism

Malcolm X advocated patronizing your own business, thereby circulating your own money in your own community. He believed that economic empowerment was intrinsically related to the overall freedom of black people. Key to this goal was the acquisition of land.

2. Self-Development and Self-Reliance—Capitalism

The Reverend Joseph Jackson believed that all efforts toward economic and social justice must lead to the idea of community. Jackson advocated that the task of the Christian is to make society the beloved community of God. Unlike Malcolm, he believed in the good of America. Further, he believed that blacks could not afford to continue to focus on what whites are not doing for blacks. Rather, blacks should focus on examining their efforts and making full use of their resources. He asserted that blacks should become producers and profit makers, not primary consumers and protestors.

3. Democratic Socialist

Dr. Martin Luther King Jr. a social prophet, grounded his mission for economic empowerment in a vision he called "Beloved Community." He advocated radical economic reform at the individual level and societal level. Thus, he believed that individually we should see our financial responsibility as a sacred responsibility, and the government and other social institutions should correct the problems of unemployment, underemployment, and job discrimination. He placed strong emphasis on the government and its social institution's role in making these corrections rather than the transformation of the black perspective about self-development.[78]

Peter J. Paris notes that it was generally agreed among black churches that the economic standing of the race was directly proportioned to the level of educational and moral development level. So improvement in the latter would result in improvement in the former. Although black economic enterprising began with the beginning of the black church, it has only become a high priority recently. This may or may not be an offspring of the mild emphasis on minority enterprises by the local, state, and federal government due to affirmative action programs. It may be an offspring of the exposure of blacks to the corporate culture, thus raising their expectations. The direct cause has not been studied.

However, the conscience of the black church as a respondent to the needs of the people it serves evolves from its Christian mandate as well as its legacy grounded in its history.[79]

Twenty-first century churches are experiencing a new wave of spiritualism and a fast approaching toddler mind-set of "what's in it for me?" There are also many distracting societal issues, some of which are major, that are giving rationale for individuals as well as churches to rethink and assess their need for traditionalism. Many churches are finding that their congregations are more diverse than mono-denominational in their religious beliefs and spirituality. Thus, some are struggling to continue tradition, some are catering to the diversity through creative means, and some find themselves drowning in a stormy sea of change.

Carlyle Stewart III speaks to these circumstances indicating that in order for churches to progress, they must develop programs that meet the needs of its members and the larger community it serves. Further, the programs need not be biblical or spiritual in the traditional sense, but they should offer people positive opportunities to transform their existential situation. "What can be more spiritual than helping cultivate a means for feeding themselves through employment? By developing creative programs that speak to a variety of human needs, the Church re-establishes itself as a spiritual center of the community it serves."[80]

Most middle-class churches are located in communities where the need for a helping hand is the greatest. It would be unconscionable for the members who consider themselves socioeconomically secure to not find creative and effective ways to respond to the socioeconomic needs that are prevalent surrounding their churches. McMickle likened these members to the words of the prophet Amos in Amos 6, condemning the leisure class of his nation, Israel, for interest in the plight of the disadvantaged. Amos contended that the consequence would be Israel suffering at the hands of the Assyrians and later the Babylonians.[81]

It is a generally accepted notion among the leaders of black churches that the black middle-class church must challenge its congregations to seize the vision of service. Some years ago, as blacks were coming into their own economically, little thought was being given to the blight that was being created. The focus of mission became that of service to those in need abroad. With the help of the Martin Luther King Jr. era, the government (federal, state, and local) began servicing the needs of the poor. However, a few churches with enlightened leadership seized a vision and utilized governmental programs as a way of getting involved in servicing the needs of the poor at home.

Carlyle Stewart asserts that mainline denominations in predominantly black urban communities have not grown because they have failed to develop outreach, which addresses the real needs of the community residents. Further, it is important to develop and maintain a balance between in-reach and outreach. The success of the church in these matters is based on how effectively the church can demonstrate love, truth, and justice.[82]

Woven throughout these models is the sense that assisting the less fortunate coincides with helping "self, individually and collectively." Moreover, there are spiritual and moral obligations that support these attitudes.

> And there was a certain beggar named Lazarus, which was laid at his gates, full of sores. (Luke 16:20 King James Version)

The mandate is clear, according to McMickle, "If the black middle-class Church is to be responsive to the needs that exist in the inner-city areas where such churches are located, responsible stewardship is a necessary component." In other words, the haves in the community, the black middle class, must be willing to share their economic resources with the have-nots—inner-city poor neighborhoods.

A critical examination of Luke 16 casts a dark shadow over the attitudes and behaviors of black middle-class congregations in regard to their stewardship to poor inner-city communities. Black middle-class congregations are challenged by this biblical text at the heart of their level of commitment to share their financial resources to aide in the uplifting of inner-city neighborhoods where black middle-class congregations reside.

Pastors and church leaders in black middle-class congregations must lead the membership to recognize that the church's mission involves discipleship and stewardship. As the church of Jesus Christ, we are called to act on behalf of others, especially on behalf of those less fortunate than ourselves, and one such action is our stewardship in support of the poor. While today, stewardship in the church is distorted by the influence of the prosperity gospel, we must not become afraid to teach members of black middle-class congregations to increase their level of giving for the cause of helping our brothers and sisters in poor inner-city neighborhoods as an integral part of our Christian stewardship.

In order for a black middle-class congregation to accept the mandate of its Christian responsibility to the have-nots and develop a ministry of economic empowerment to poor inner-city neighborhoods, the membership must adopt the words of Jesus in Luke 12:48 (HCSB):

> Much will be required of everyone who has been given much. And even more will be expected of the one who has been entrusted with more.

Conclusion

According to McMickle, C. Eric Lincoln provided an insightful view on the response of black middle-class churches to the poor inner-city neighborhoods outside the church doors in his book *The Black Church in the African-American Experience* when he said:

> One advantage that many Black churches have is the fact that the majority of them are still located in the ghetto°... Black Churches can take advantage of their location and begin the difficult task of organizing these deprived inner-city communities and providing a political voice and community infrastructure, whether they will do so remains to be seen.

As Christians, we cannot ignore the inner-city poor and hold on to the ethical credence of the Christian gospel. The example of Jesus Christ teaches us that to be a Christian is to love one's neighbor and that involves becoming our brothers and sisters keeper.

Black middle-class congregations must not become so satisfied with job, status, and family that we are blinded to the problems existing in surrounding poor inner-city communities. As the people of God, not only should we pray for justice, but pray for justice for all. In other words, blacks who have moved up in their educational and economic standing in what appears to be an affluent society and who subscribe to Christian principles should be involved in helping to assist those who are suffering serious social and economic deprivation. Thus, it is not unreasonable to conclude that as the economic status rises within black middle-class churches, ministries of economic empowerment to poor inner-city neighborhoods should increase.

With closing the gap between the haves and the have-nots in mind, the ministry of black middle-class churches in the twenty-first century should be that no community is left behind due to a lack of economic resources.

Endnotes

Chapter 1

Empowering the Poor: Biblical, Theological, Historical and Theoretical Foundations for a Ministry of Economic Empowerment

1   Nelson, Thomas. *What Does the Bible Say About°.....: The Ultimate A to Z Resource*. Nashville, TN: Thomas Nelson, Inc., 2001, 168.

2   Walton, Rus. *Biblical Solutions to Contemporary Problems: A Handbook*. Brentwood, TN: Wolgemuth and Hyatt Publishers, Inc., 1988.

3   Ibid.

5   McMickle, Marvin A. *Preaching to the Black Middle Class: Words of Challenge, Words of Hope*. Valley Forge, PA: Judson Press, 2000, 57.

6   Jeavons, Thomas H. and Rebekah Burch Basinger. *Growing Givers' Hearts, Treating Fundraising as Ministry*. San Francisco, CA: Jossey-Bass, 2000, 100–101.

7   Weems, Lovett H. Jr. *John Wesley's Message Today*. Nashville, TN: Abingdon Press, 1991.

8   Niebuhr, Reinhold. *Moral Man and Immoral Society.* New York, NY: Charles Scribner's Sons, 1960, 17.

9   Ibid., 121, 127.

10   Bacik, James. *Contemporary Theologians.* Chicago, IL: The Thomas More Press, 1989, 130.

11   Ibid.

12   Ibid., 131.

13   Ibid.

14   Ibid., 169.

15   Ibid.

16   Ibid., 172.

17   Ibid.

18   Ibid., 174.

19   Ibid.

20   Mollegen Jr., A. T. *Three Attitudes toward Giving.* http://members. aol.com/stewardshp/3paradms.htm.

21   Grimm, Eugene. *Generous People.* Nashville, TN: Abingdon Press, 1992, 40–42.

22   Ibid.

23 United Methodist Foundation of Detroit Annual conference, The Stewardship Journey. http://www.comnet.org/umf2.

24 Grimm, *Generous People*, 19.

25 United Methodist Foundation of Detroit Annual conference, The Stewardship Journey. http://www.comnet.org/umf3.

26 Hoge, Dean R., Charles Zech, Patrick McNamara, and Michael J. Donahue. *Money Matters: Personal Giving In American Churches.* Louisville, KY: Westminster John Knox Press, 1996, 146.

27 Jeavon, *Growing Givers' Hearts, Treating Fundraising as Ministry*, 115.

28 Toler, Stan and Elmer Towns. *Developing a Giving Church.* Kansas City, MO: Beacon Hill Press of Kansas City, 1999, 61–62.

29 Callahan, Kennon L. *Giving and Stewardship in an Effective Church, a Guide for Every Member.* San Francisco, CA: Jossey-Bass, 1992, 9–12.

30 Grimm, *Generous People*, 105–109, 115.

31 Herrington, Jim, Mike Bonem, and James Furr. *Leading Congregational Change.* San Francisco, CA: Jossey-Bass, 2000, 29.

Chapter 2

Guides for Church Leadership in Affecting Congregational Change Toward Economic Empowerment

32 Ibid., 30–31.

33 Ibid., 31–32.

34 Ibid., 34–36

35 Ibid., 41.

36 Ibid., 41–42.

37 Ibid., 41.

38 Ibid., 50

39 Ibid., 50–52

40 Ibid., 61–62

41 Ibid., 62–65

42 Ibid., 64.

43 Ibid., 68.

44 Ibid., 70–71.

45 Ibid., 75.

46 Ibid., 78, 83.

47 Ibid., 85.

48 Ibid.

49 Christian Century Foundation. "Churches Lag in Giving to Benevolence Funds Research." Empty Tomb Inc., January 31, 2001, 1.

50 Nelson, Alan and Gene Appel. *How to Change Your Church (Without Killing It)*. Nashville, TN: W. Publishing Group, 2000, 100.

51 Blackaby, Henry and Richard Blackaby, "What is Spiritual Leadership?" *Christianity Today International Leadership Journal* (Winter 2003): 3–6. Taken from Henry and Richard Blackaby, *Spiritual Leadership* (Broadman and Holman, 2001). http:// christinitytoday.com.

52 Ibid.

53 Ibid., 2.

54 Ibid.

55 Domokos, Robert L. "Effective Leadership." *Faith Pulpit* (September 1990), 1–3. http:www.faith.edu/pulpit.2.

56 Ibid.

57 Ibid.

58 Ibid.

59 Nelson and Appel, *How to Change Your Church (Without Killing It)*, 101.

60 Bennis, Warren, *Learning to Lead: A Workbook on Becoming a Leader*, 1997

61 Coutts, Peter. "Leadership vs. Management." PCC (Presbyterian Church in Canada) Leadership Site. http://www.presbyterian.ca.2

62 Nelson and Appel, *How to Change Your Church (Without Killing It),* 101.

63 Krejcir, Richard. "A Primer on How to Lead and Manage a Church." Into the Word Ministries. http://Christianity.com.6.

64 Hybels, Bill. "Finding Your Leadership Style: Ten Different Ways to Lead God's People." *Christianity Today International Leadership Journal,* (Winter 1998): 1–9. http://christianity.com

65 Ibid.

66 Ibid.

67 Ibid.

68 Ibid.

69 Ibid.

70 Ibid., 5

71 Ibid., 6

72 Ibid.

73 Ibid.

74 Ibid.

75 Krejcir, "A Primer on How to Lead and Manage a Church."

76 Herrington, Bonen, and Furr, *Leading Congregational Change,* 16–27.

Chapter 3

Models of Ministries Engaged in Economic Empowerment

77 Paris, Peter J. *The Social Teaching of the Black Churches*. Philadelphia, PA: Fortress Press, 1985, 18.

78 Malone Jr, Dr. Walter. *From Holy Power to Holy Profits: The Black Church and Community Economic Empowerment*. Chicago, IL: African American Images, 1994, 53–62.

79 Paris, *The Social Teaching of the Black Churches*, 69–70.

80 Stewart III, Carlyle F. *African American Church Growth: 12 Principles for Prophetic Ministry*. Nashville, TN: Abingdon Press, 1994, 141.

81 McMickle, *Preaching to the Black Middle Class: Words of Challenge, Words of Hope,*58.

82 Stewart III, *African American Church Growth: 12 Principles for Prophetic Ministry*, 129–121.

Bibliography

Bacik, James. *Contemporary Theologians*. Chicago, IL: The Thomas More Press, 1989.

Blackaby, Henry and Richard Blackaby. *What Is Spiritual Leadership; Christianity Today International Leadership Journal*. (Winter 2003): 3–6. Taken from Henry and Richard Blackaby. *Spiritual Leadership*. Broadman and Holman, 2001. http://christianitytoday.com

Callahan, Kennon L. *Giving and Stewardship in an Effective Church: A Guide for Every Member*. San Francisco, CA: Jossey-Bass, 1992.

Christian Century Foundation. *Churches Lag on Giving to Benevolence Funds*. Empty Tomb Inc., Research. January 31, 2001.

Domokos, Robert L. *Effective Pastoral Leadership*. Faith Pulpit. September 1990. http://www.faith.edu/pulpits.

Grimm, Eugene. *Generous People*. Nashville, TT: Abingdon Press, 1992.

Herrington, Jim, Mike Bonem and James Furr. *Leading Congregational Change*. San Francisco, CA: Jossey-Bass, 2000.

Hoge, Dean R., Charles Zech, Patrick McNamara, and Michael J. Donahue. *Money Matters: Personal Giving in American Churches*. Louisville, KY: Westminster John Knox Press, 1996.

Hybels, Bill. "Funding Your Leadership Style: Ten Different Ways to Lead God's People." *Christianity Today International Leadership Journal*. (Winter 1998). http:// christianitytoday.com

Jeavons, Thomas H. and Rebekah Burch Basinger. *Growing Givers' Hearts Treating Fundraising as Ministry*. San Francisco, CA: Jossey-Bass, 2000.

Krejcir, Richard. *A Primer on How to Lead and Manage the Church. Into Thy Word Ministries*. http://www. christianity. com.

Krejcir, Richard. *The Leadership Challenge*. Into Thy Word Ministries. http://www.christianity. Com.

Malone Jr., Dr. Walter. *From Holy Power to Holy Profits: The Black Church and Community Economic Empowerment.* Chicago, IL: African American Images, 1994.

McMickle, Marvin A. *Preaching to the Black Middle Class: Words of Challenge, Words of Hope.* Valley Forge, PA: Judson Press, 2000.

Miller, Kevin. *Heart and Soul: Christianity Today International Leadership Journal.* Fall 1998. http://christianitytoday.com.

Mollegen, A. T. Jr. *Three Attitudes Toward Giving.* http// members.aol.com/stewardship/3paradms.htm.

Nelson, Alan and Gene Appel. *How to Change Your Church (Without Killing It).* Nashville, TN: W Publishing Group, 2000.

Nelson, Thomas, *What Does the Bible Say About°... The Ultimate A to Z Resource.* Nashville, TN: Thomas Nelson, Inc., 2001.

Niebuhr, Reinhold. *Moral Man and Immoral Society.* New York, NY: Charles Scribner's Sons, 1960.

Paris, Peter J. *The Social Teaching of the Black Churches.* Philadelphia, PA: Fortress Press, 1985.

Stewart, Carlyle, F. III. *African American Church Growth: 12 Principles for Prophetic Ministry.* Nashville, TN: Abingdon Press, 1994.

United Methodist Foundation of the Detroit Annual Conference. *The Stewardship Journey.* http://www.comnet. org/umf.

Walton, Rus. *Biblical Solutions to Contemporary Problems: A Handbook.* Brentwood, TN: Wolgemuth and Hyatt, Publishers, Inc., 1988.

Weems, Lovett H. Jr. *John Wesley's Message Today.* Nashville, TN: Abingdon Press, 1991.

West, Cornel. *Race Matters.* Boston, MA: Beacon Press, 1993.

About the Author

Dr. John F. Green, an ordained itinerant elder in the African Methodist Episcopal Church, is a well-respected preacher and teacher; a church-builder and administrator; a community activist; and a theological leader. He has a demonstrated passion for realizing the church's commission for outreach to those who are struggling to survive the myriad complexities and challenges of present-day culture and in need of spiritual, physical, and/or emotional healing.

Dr. Green currently serves as president-dean of Turner Theological Seminary, the African Methodist Episcopal Church (AMEC) affiliate of the Interdenominational Theological Seminary, Atlanta, Georgia. He accepted the assignment to executive leadership in this ecumenical academic setting after serving as the senior pastor at Bethel African Methodist Episcopal Church in Tallahassee, Florida, for twelve years. This followed twenty-four years of parish ministry, primarily in the Eleventh Episcopal District of the AME Church, including pastoral leadership for Hurst Chapel AME Church, Orlando, Florida; Hurst Chapel AME Church in Winter Haven, Florida; and Allen Temple AME Church,

Tampa, Florida. His success in these charges resulted from the unabashed manner in which he demonstrates his skills as a servant leader.

A native of Kissimmee, Florida, Dr. Green is an intellectual and enthusiastic conversationalist. He holds a Doctor of Ministry Degree from the United Theological Seminary, Dayton, Ohio; a Master of Divinity Degree from the Interdenominational Theological Center, Turner Theological Seminary, Atlanta, Georgia; and a Bachelor of Science Degree from the University of South Florida, Tampa, Florida.

His concerns and innate willingness to serve throughout his career as a pastor, teacher, and administrator in the theological context have earned him numerous awards, including being recognized by the Tallahassee Branch of the NAACP as a Black Achiever and honored as a Leadership Pacesetter by Leadership Tallahassee of the Tallahassee Chamber of Commerce.

Dr. Green is the husband of Phyllis McClendon Green, the Episcopal Supervisor of the Seventh Episcopal District, AMEC, and the proud father of a daughter, Courtney S. Green, a graduate of Florida A&M University currently pursuing a Master's Degree in Integrated Marketing with aspirations for a career in public relations and communications.

73586792R00067

Made in the USA
Columbia, SC
13 July 2017